Look Back at Old Aberbeeg & Llanhilleth

Ray Morris
& Malcolm Thomas

Foreword by
Trevor Wilde, M.B.E.

Volume 1

Old Bakehouse Publications

Abertillery

© Ray Morris & Malcolm Thomas

First published June 2001

ISBN 1 874538 97 2

Published in the U.K. by
Old Bakehouse Publications
Church Street,
Abertillery, Gwent NP13 1EA
Telephone: 01495 212600 Fax: 01495 216222
www.mediamaster.co.uk/oldbakebooks

Made and printed in the UK
by J.R. Davies (Printers) Ltd.

Foreword

by
Trevor Wilde, M.B.E.

To begin at the beginning I must take you back to 1917-18. I remember my mother sitting me on the counter at Edmunds store when I was about four years of age. That store later became Dowie Davies's billiard hall, and later still, Lou Poole's. It was of course known as Manchester House.

Here at Aberbeeg, we had the home of Welsh beers at Webbs Brewery. They always had a brew at weekends, and the smell of the hops rose up to our Sunday School rooms at the Prims chapel up on the hill. You could still smell it on a Monday morning, but it was then mixed with the burning smell of horse hooves at Jim Bolt's smithey, where he would be fitting a horse out with new shoes.

The Whitsun walks were a great feature of village life. After walking and singing our marching tunes, to Llanhilleth and back, we had sandwiches and cake at the chapel. Then down to the local football field for games. A favourite game for the girls was the first to kiss Mr. Will Legge, who was at the other end of the field. The prize was threepence!

My memory is crowded with characters and occasions far too numerous to mention. However this volume is so well compiled and so beautifully illustrated that any further quote from me would be a waste of time and space. And so I will end with a few lines by John Keats.

A thing of beauty is a joy forever,
It will never pass into nothingness.

For such are my memories of my Aberbeeg and the surrounding areas.

T. Wilde.

Contents

Introduction

t is more than seven years since a book was last published providing a detailed photographic history of the districts of Aberbeeg and Llanhilleth. Therefore, as we are now progressing through the early years of a new century, this might be the time to take another look at the people, places and events that graced the previous one hundred years. To do this, we have accumulated and assembled a collection of more than two hundred previously unpublished photographs of the area for all to enjoy. Since the 1970s the changes to *'Welsh Valley Life'*, its atmospheres and environment have been dramatic to say the least, these facts would naturally be far more obvious to older generations and those who have migrated to other parts.

Aberbeeg has received particular attention in this respect and a village that once accommodated an important railway junction, an extensive brewery, a colliery and a cluster of shops is now a place that bears no resemblance whatsoever; a major road link being the main culprit for that. Llanhilleth too has suffered a similar fate although perhaps to a slightly lesser degree, for at least, as locals will know, one can still collect one's old age pension locally, purchase some items of food and find places of worship and entertainment with much of the town's original housing being retained. The most notable change is possibly the removal of any evidence of coal-mining here, Llanhilleth's colliery closing in 1969 with the loss of many valuable jobs and at one time employing up to 1900 men. Coal-mining of course was once the great provider of *'jobs for life'* and despite all the dangers that came with it, it still held the attraction for thousands over the years. By the end of the twentieth century however, all had changed, with something just in the region of 150 miners still employed in the whole of South Wales. In fact, in the year 2000, statistics informed us that the most dangerous occupation throughout the United Kingdom was no longer mining, but surprisingly, the fishing industry!

This latest book embraces a number of topics which should be of interest to a number of generations, young and old and there is a wide variety of photographs to be savoured. For more mature readers there are many familiar names and family businesses to recall, such as Webbs Brewery, whose aromas could be relished all over Aberbeeg and beyond; then there was Ron Jones and his bus company, with characters such as *'Sarge'* at the wheel and Thomas's the baker whose delicious smells were to some, a welcome alternative to the nearby alcoholic emissions from the aforementioned nineteenth-century brewery. Some ancient buildings have survived such as Christchurch, Aberbeeg Hospital and Llanhilleth's Workingmen's Institute, all of which belong to almost a century ago. Some of those which have not survived, yet still remembered by many include the Hanbury Hotel, the railway stations at both Aberbeeg and Llanhilleth and not forgetting The Playhouse where one could enjoy professional stage productions or simply sit in the *'One and Nines'*.

There are past tragedies to think about too, like Ron Jones losing three of his brothers in an air disaster in 1950, underground fatalities (thankfully few) in the Aberbeeg and Llanhilleth collieries and the case of poor Billy Poole in the 1920s. He was a young lad who did what many might have done in their youth, whilst living near a busy railway line. Playing one day, he failed to escape the path of a train and suffered severe leg injuries which resulted in the local surgeon carrying out amputation on the kitchen table in Billy's home in Railway Terrace. The story does not end there, for it is said that his family were so distraught, that it was decided to bury the amputated leg in the family grave in St. Illtyd's churchyard. The lad survived the surgery well and went on to work for many years in the colliery lamp room, having been fitted with a false limb. When he finally passed away however, he was actually buried at Christchurch thus having the curious claim to be resting in two graves!

Our thanks are extended to those who have kindly loaned some of their own photographs and accompanying memories and of course to doyen Mr. Trevor Wilde for his considerate foreword.

CHAPTER 1

Views of Aberbeeg

1. The first photograph in this book should be recognizable mainly to the more mature residents of the Aberbeeg area. It was taken outside Thomas's shop in Commercial Road and includes Olive Parry, Charlie Abraham, Reg Butler, Harry Parry, Percy Poole, Stan Butler and Mr. Williams (Brynithel).

2. A mountainside view overlooking the valley that captures a few of Aberbeeg's landmarks. On the right, amidst the trees, can be seen the church tower with the hospital close by. Set down in the valley is the stack belonging to the former Webbs Brewery, which provided the rich aroma so familiar in the district for a century and a half.

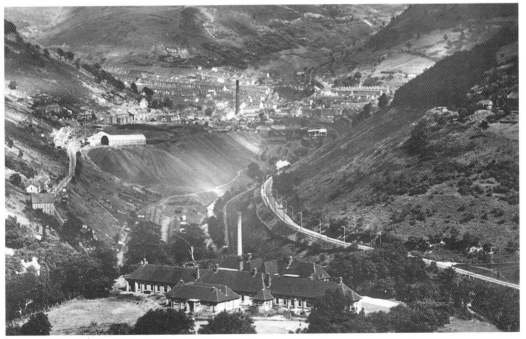

3. Another view from the mountainside showing some more distant scenes such as the Primitive Methodist Chapel and Warm Turn. To the right of the picture is Victoria Road leading to Six Bells, with its conspicuous colliery workings still in place.

4. This particular picture dates from about 1912, the identifying features being the old steep bridge leading from Aberbeeg to Thomas's Emporium and bakery and the original engine sheds which were closed in 1919. Ty'r Graig school, seen in the lower right, was at this time, a modern centre of education having been opened in 1912 with capacity for 780 pupils.

5. A scene similar to the previous picture except that the old steep bridge has gone, to be replaced by the nineteen-arched construction, still there today. Also gone are the original engine sheds, with new buildings appearing in the lower right of the photograph, these being opened in April 1919 to cope with the additional railway traffic now being seen in Aberbeeg.

6./7. Two views belonging to the 1920s and 1930s from Pantddu that overlook the valley and Aberbeeg. Through the ages the name 'Aberbeeg' has been recorded in various versions such as Aberbyg and Aberbyg Bridge during the 16th and 17th centuries before settling at Aberbeeg in about 1790. The name is derived from the Welsh 'Aber' meaning mouth of river or stream and 'Big' the name of an old brook flowing into the river Ebbw Fawr.

8. This is a scene at Brewery Row taken whilst the area was in the process of being refurbished in the late sixties or early seventies. This row of houses was built in the nineteenth century by the Webb family as accommodation for their brewery workers. Originally known as Crooks Row (the name probably being adopted from a Mr. John Crook who had married Miss Elizabeth Webb), the name was changed to Brewery Row in about 1900.

9. The 1980s, and the centre of Aberbeeg is beginning to take on a new look with the construction of the new road to Cwm. The building on the lower left is the former shop Manchester House and the only buildings now remaining are the houses of Brewery Row.

10. New Woodland Terrace looking in a southerly direction sometime during the 1930s and the cameraman of the day seems to attract the attention of the local residents.

11. Local residents and former customers will remember this centrepiece of Aberbeeg, namely the Hanbury Hotel, adjacent to the Webbs Brewery. The impressive-looking building is seen here in the late 1890s, shortly after having been acquired at auction by the Webb brothers Richard and Tom, then owners of the acclaimed Webbs Wine and Spirit Company.

12./13. Two very early photographs of Graig View, certainly pre-1912 as Ty'r Graig school has yet to be built. Close examination of the lower picture will show the houses of Brynawel Terrace still under construction, with scaffolding in position and awaiting addition of some windows; work has also just commenced on another two houses to the left.

14. Arael Hill with the railway signal box and a few more buildings no longer to be seen in the district. In the foreground are the end houses of Riverside Row and Henry Kibby's grocery store, a family-run business which in later years developed into a national supermarket chain. To assist younger readers, the small building in the front right of the picture is now the site of the workshop belonging to the Flyover Garage.

15. Glandwr Baptist Chapel a well-known place of nonconformist worship as it looked in 1908. The Baptist cause here can be traced back to the aspirations of local man Mr. David Phillips, who began using his own home as a temporary meeting place in 1821. This was to continue for a number of years under the careful eye of Rev. William Thomas of Blaenau Gwent until 1837, when sufficient support and membership allowed the building of a chapel proper. The Phillips family were the main benefactors and Glandwr, at a cost of £500, opened its doors in the year 1838, with the Rev. John Davies of Llandyssul as its first pastor; this is one of the few chapels still serving the community in the district.

16. 'Ye Olde Bridge Aberbeeg' is the caption on this original postcard of 1905. In the shop doorway is Mrs. Emma Twissell who, with her husband Herbert ran a popular shop for many years. Mrs. Twissell served her customers' requirements for chinaware and fancy goods whilst her husband was the local hairdresser.

17. As already mentioned, Webbs Brewery was quite a significant employer in the district for almost 150 years, founded by a Staffordshire family in the early part of the nineteenth century. The 1960s saw a period of tough competition and mergers within the brewing industry, with many of the smaller firms being absorbed by the more sizeable national companies. The Aberbeeg site was taken over by Northern Breweries Ltd. in 1960, and the familiar trademark, as seen on the roof of the building when it was under ownership of Welsh Brewers in 1981, began to disappear forever. Whilst brewing actually ceased in 1969, the plant was used as a distribution centre until final closure in 1988.

18. Perched in a commanding position overlooking the Ebbw Valley is Christ Church. It is pictured here during the final days of its construction as evidenced by the builders' scaffolding which is still in position. When Reverend Daniel Felix (former curate of Abergavenny) was inducted as incumbent of the parish of Llanhilleth in 1895, the area of Aberbeeg, with its population of around a thousand souls was actually a part of three different parishes, namely Llanhilleth, Abertillery and Penmaen; at that time and for centuries past, the parish church of Llanhilleth was St. Illtyd's on the mountain top at Brynithel.

In 1891 a public hall was erected in Aberbeeg which was also used for divine worship and although served by the rector of Llanhilleth, it was actually in the parish of Penmaen. Further down the valley was Crumlin, with a population of around 2,000 residing mainly in the parish of Penmaen yet with a small proportion, some 200, in the parish of Llanhilleth. In this instance whilst the mission room at Crumlin was served by the clergy of Penmaen, it really stood in Llanhilleth.

This situation was deemed to be very confusing and unnecessary to the rector of Llanhilleth and Rev. Gower of Penmaen, who both agreed that new boundaries were needed as soon as possible. After much deliberation and negotiation with the Church authorities, the new boundaries were finally declared in 1897 and remain as such to this day. Some ten years after this event, the ever-enthusiastic Rev. Felix was keen to see a new and enlarged place of worship for the residents of Aberbeeg; consequently he procured a measure of land on the hillside, a gracious gift from the late J.C. Hanbury of Pontypool renown.

The rectory was constructed first, to house the vicar and his wife with work commencing on the church soon after; the official dedication taking place in November 1909. In true late 14th century style and with seating for 400 worshippers, the total cost of Christ Church amounted to a precise figure of £6278.58. This was a vast sum for the period yet much of the funding was provided by the parishioners themselves, with help from a number of local colliery owners such as Budds, Lancasters and Partridge Jones. The largest contribution however came from Rev. Felix and his wife, who were of a notable wealthy disposition, they providing a sizeable £1,400 towards the project.

Reverend Felix was known to be an ardent opponent of strong drink in the district, and not all financial assistance offered by local employers was found to be acceptable. Typically, when John Edgar Webb, owner of Webbs Brewery wished to donate a much needed church organ, the Reverend flatly refused, thus maintaining his uncompromising principles to the letter; consequently, the said organ was gratefully accepted by St. Michael's in Abertillery. In December 1911, by an Order in Council, Christ Church was substituted for that of St. Illtyd's at Brynithel, as the new parish church.

Daniel Felix was to serve the parish for a total of 35 years until 1930, he also being responsible for the building of St. Marks church in Llanhilleth, which is to be seen later in this book. Christ Church is still as imposing on the hillside in Aberbeeg as it was 90 years ago, the building surviving whereas most else has disappeared from the valley floor. As with any long-established place of worship, the costs of maintenance and repairs are a constant burden and any contribution to the upkeep of Christ Church is most welcome, large or small.

Inset

Rev. Robert Prescott, rector of the parish of Llanhilleth.

After working for 35 years as an electrician, Mr. Prescott entered St. Michael's Theological College, Llandaff, Cardiff for training for ministry within the Church in Wales. He attained a Diploma in Practical Theology at the University of Wales, Cardiff, in 1995 and was ordained Deacon. In 1996 he was ordained Priest where he served the Parish of Abertillery, Cwmtillery and Six Bells before his Induction as Rector of the Parish of Llanhilleth on 20th May 1999.

19. Whilst official passenger services through Aberbeeg were withdrawn in April 1962, in March that year a 'steam special' was organized by the Stephenson Locomotive Society which is pictured here packed with railway enthusiasts. The train is facing towards Blaina and in busier days, travellers would change platforms here for a journey on to Cwm and Ebbw Vale.

20. Aberbeeg was an all important junction in the railway network of the Western Valley where the lines branched off to Ebbw Vale in one direction and Brynmawr in the other. The passenger service from Newport, as far as Blaina, was opened in 1850 by the Monmouthshire Railway and Canal Company with two trains per day in each direction; such were the primitive designs of track and locomotives of the day, the journey took a leisurely 1 hour and 45 minutes! The route to Ebbw Vale was opened in 1852, with trains from Newport initially being divided at Aberbeeg, one half being pulled as far as Blaina, the other as far as Ebbw Vale thus allowing passengers to remain in their section of the train.

21. What is nowadays the Glandwr Industrial Estate, was once the site of Aberbeeg's engine shed and maze of railway track. First planned in 1913 as an urgent requirement for the high volume of steam locomotives then working the valley, the building was delayed due to the advent of war; the new building eventually opened in June 1919 with capacity for the care for 36 engines. In its heyday more than 150 men, including the crews were employed at Aberbeeg shed, the steam engines being fed with some 400 tons of coal a week. The end of an era came with closure in 1964.

22. The name of Dr. Beeching, chairman of the British Railways Board was infamous in the 1960s through implementing sweeping cuts in the country's passenger rail services. The Western Valley network was decimated, the last official passenger train passing through Aberbeeg in April 1962. Due to the number of collieries still working in the valley, freight traffic continued for some years after, until the mining industry too suffered the same fate as the railways. A locomotive is seen at the station taking on water with Mr. Bob Fowler, a local railwayman stood on the right.

23. This is one of the rarer photographs of Aberbeeg Station, taken in about 1880. The train seen here is at the down platform from Ebbw Vale and the driver leaning out of the cab is Mr. Arthur Hill Poole whose granddaughter Elizabeth still resides in Aberbeeg aged 91. The original owners of the valley line, The Monmouthshire Railway and Canal Company ran into some financial difficulties by the 1870s, which caught the eye of the mighty Great Western who agreed to lease much of the Monmouth's undertakings. Complete amalgamation came in 1880 and with sizeable investment and increased business, much of which came from the coal companies, fortunes returned.

The GWR continued to manage the services until nationalization in 1948.

24. A rare occasion some ninety years ago when railway staff and fellow workers were allowed to 'trespass' the line at Aberbeeg for a special group photograph. The gentleman in the front and probably uncomfortably sat on the rail, dons a bowler hat, indicating that he was a gaffer of some sort.

25. More railway nostalgia as a goods train is pictured on its way to Ebbw Vale steelworks with a load of iron-ore during the 1960s. A few more former landmarks since disappeared include River Row (once occupied by sinkers working at the old original colliery), and Kibby's shop with some adjacent ...

26. Only during the late 1990s did Aberbeeg finally lose its Post Office after more than 120 years. This is the office in the year 1902, it being a sub-office of the larger premises at Six Bells. This was an important place for news and communication before the arrival of public telephones and during the time of this photograph, the postmaster was Mr. Thomas Jones.

27./28. Above are two photographs from the 1890s of William Thomas and his wife Rowena that help report some humble beginnings in Aberbeeg. William Thomas was born of farming stock in Pembrokeshire in 1851, later moving to Newport, Gwent to take up employment as a butcher's apprentice at the age of 14. He subsequently married a lady, Miss Rowena Rowlands and decided to move to Aberbeeg where they opened their own butcher's shop, complete with living accommodation.

In the mid 1880s a young man by the name of William Evans, also from Pembroke, came to live with the couple and work in the shop. Evans, full of business acumen, persuaded the more cautious Thomas that they should form a partnership and develop their commercial interests further afield. Consequently, Thomas loaned Evans the sum of £238, at an alarming interest rate of 50%, probably as a sure bet of getting his money back one day. The chosen trade of this new partnership was the manufacture of soft drinks which were distributed from a works at Porth, in the Rhondda Valley and under the brand name of Thomas and Evans. Whilst Evans was keen to further expand and exploit a fast-growing market for temperate liquid refreshment, Thomas, ever cautious, would not agree to these ideas and the partnership was dissolved by mutual agreement.

On reflection, there may have been a little lack of foresight and confidence at the time, as the soft drinks business was snapped up by the Corona company, later to become one of the nation's best-loved 'pop' producers. What became of William Evans has yet to be researched, but the Thomas's further expanded their Aberbeeg business as a family concern selling groceries and the baking of bread, Mrs. Thomas concentrating her efforts in the millinery trade. So it was, that a nationally-known product was to have found its origins in a butcher's shop in Aberbeeg.

29. A further picture from the Thomas family with Lionel (centre) and his two sons Carl and Garry. Lionel, born in 1881 and one of twins, joined the business upon leaving school and took it over when his father William died in 1925. There followed some twenty years of continuous expansion, and besides the bakery and millinery shop in Aberbeeg, premises were opened in Llanhilleth, Oakdale, Newbridge and Pontllanfraith. The two sons seen here also joined the business for a number of years after war service, until a general decline in trade necessitated the closing of the Emporium and the disposal of the outlying shops. The brothers' involvement did however continue with Carl retaining the bakery and Garry and his wife, the Llanhilleth shop. Lionel Thomas died in 1968 and his two sons in 1976, thus bringing to an end yet another family business in the area.

30. Another view of old Aberbeeg from a different direction and looking towards Warm Turn. The scene is from the mid 1930s when the district was a hive of activity.

31./32. Constructing a new road junction between Aberbeeg and Six Bells was no mean feat as illustrated in these two photographs showing the amount of rock that needed to be removed.

33. More mature readers and residents will recall the most appealing and mouth-watering aroma that would drift onto the street from the bakery in Woodland Terrace and above, is local baker Joe Day. The bakery was founded by his parents Fred and Eleanor in about 1910 who later formed a partnership with Jim James of Chepstow in the early 1920s. Successive members of the families ran the business as James and Day until closure in 1957, brought on by stiff competition from the larger companies.

34. A member of the bakery staff Tony Verrier is seen with the delivery van in the 1950s and readers may also recall such names as Emlyn Williams, Wally Clarke, Carl Blackwell, Bill Tunkin, Ken Harvey, Colin Wilde, John Maggs, Gwyneth Wilde, Cissy Vaughan and Winnie Lewis, all of whom were employed at the bakery at one time or another. The founder, Fred Day died in 1941 aged 76 whilst his wife Eleanor lived to a ripe old age of 92, passing on in 1950.

35. A former popular 'watering hole' was the Ivorites, originally known as the Ivorites Arms. Owned by the Rhymney Brewery Company, the pub closed during the mid 1960s as the population of Aberbeeg began to dwindle; regulars will remember the last landlord as Mr. Albert Francombe, and all that remains here today is the railings seen in the foreground.

36. A Public House steeped in history is the Carpenter's Arms near the church at St. Illtyds. Pictured in about 1904 with an ornate porch at the entrance, the inn was offering Burton and Bristol Ales, drawn from the wood and ample stabling for one's horse. The exterior appearance of the inn has now been completely renovated and bears little resemblance to this photograph.

37. A centre for relaxation and conversation in old Aberbeeg, were the benches outside the Hanbury Hotel. This picture was taken amidst the great depression of the 1930s, and yet this hotel managed to survive it all, and offer its services for a further fifty years.

38. The River Ebbw rarely poses a threat to the people of Aberbeeg but this photograph, taken during the torrential storms of December 1979, might refresh the memories of local inhabitants of Railway Terrace. A kitchen and bathroom were completely swept away and a number of houses suffered severe flood damage.

39. The scene looking northwards along Commercial Road is a quiet one in the year 1910, the only traffic being a horse waiting outside the ironmonger's shop belonging to John Edward Rowland. Also in the background are Thomas's the bakers, The Emporium and Aberbeeg School.

40. Aberbeeg Colliery as seen in about 1918. The first colliery here was opened in about 1860 by local entrepreneur William Webb and his partners Messers Spittle and Partieh who, in the 1870s, passed the business on to Powell and Sons. During the last twenty years of the colliery's life it was operated by Budd and Company, who were major exporters of valley coal from Newport and Cardiff docks; some 265 men were employed at this pit, working the Tillery Seam during its peak period of 1913. The year 1913 was also record-breaking across the whole of the South Wales coalfield with a total of 57 million tons being extracted and 233,000 miners in full employment. However there was a 'downside' to all this activity, with the price of coal averaging a mere 74 pence per ton, an underground worker at Aberbeeg in 1913 was earning just 34 pence per shift!

During the early part of 1919 the Ebbw Vale Iron and Coal Co. declared their intention to sink a completely new mine in the Aberbeeg area, the announcement being particularly welcomed as men were now returning from the war and in need of work in a civilian life. The site chosen was near the bottom of Cwm Road on the other side of the railway line and river. By the summer, work was well under way with the sinking of the first shaft to a depth of 30 yards and the construction of an engine house. By December however, bad news arrived when the company announced that operations were to be suspended indefinitely and most of the eighty workers were given notice or offered jobs elsewhere. Rumour had it that the government was proposing a profit ceiling of 6p per ton for the coal-owners thus making the opening of any new colliery uneconomical; the remains of the shaft of this pit are now completely filled in.

Aberbeeg did eventually get its new colliery but this was nearer Crumlin than Aberbeeg itself and was named Aberbeeg South, the housecoal pit of the Navigation Colliery. The pit employed an average of 200 men during its lifetime, producing some 50,000 tons of coal annually. The first Aberbeeg colliery seen above, closed in the early 1920s and Aberbeeg South closed in December 1965 with the Navigation following two years later.

41. This picture which was taken at Aberbeeg junction in the early 1960s alongside locomotive number 4650, shows two fellow railway workers. Unfortunately it was not possible to positively identify them but the choice of names given was Roy Mapp, Tony Saunders and Horace Price.

42. Signalman Terry Parsons is seen at work in the once very busy and important signal box at Aberbeeg. Whilst traffic diminished swiftly through the 1960s and '70s, this signal box remained in use until the late 1990s, controlling minimal freight to and from Ebbw Vale steelworks.

43. Any readers who may have worked or had relatives on the railway at Aberbeeg, may well recognize a few faces on this picture which was taken outside the sheds during the 1960s. In the back will be found Joe Jayne, Gwyn Hudson, Em Saunders, Harry Iles, Bill Parry, Bill Bevan and Harold Wakeley (fitter). In the front are Albert Coles, Fred Parsons, Fred Churchill, Cyril Hotham and Frank Bevan.

CHAPTER 2

Aberbeeg People & Lifestyle

44. A photograph taken outside the hospital for a special occasion and amongst the numerous dignitaries and guests are Councillor Jack Clarke, Mary Edwards, Ted Meredith and Dewi Price.

45. Where would any hospital be without the gracious help and allegiance of the League of Friends? Unfortunately it has not been possible to trace many names on this photograph and apologies are offered, however the group does include Ted Meredith J.P., Jack Brown, Mrs. Doel, Mrs. Collier, Beryl Donald, Mrs. Hanney, Mrs. Pettet and Ginny Gladfield.

46. Wherever and whenever there is mention of Aberbeeg Hospital, the name of Dr. R.W. 'Bill' Scanlon will be at the forefront. The multi-qualified former General Practitioner became the resident surgeon at the hospital with the formation of the National Health Service in 1948 until his retirement in 1965. Dr. Scanlon is seen on the left of this 1958 photograph taken during the visit of Mrs. Vijaya Pandit, sister of India's first premier, Pandit Nehru. Between Mr. Scanlon and Mrs. Pandit is another familiar face, that of Matron Body. Other members of staff include - Front: Sister Lewis, S/N Hopkins, Nurses M. Parry, G. Jaynes and Mr. D. Aubrey. Back: Nurse Collins, Sister M. Prosser, Nurse J. Judge, H. Watkins, Sister V. Poultney, E. Jenkins, G. Nash, E. Lewis, A. Morgan, Ms. Rodgers, Ms. Priddy and D. Francis.

47. The end of another era at the hospital was marked with the retirement of Matron Body. Shaking hands with Matron is Sister Lewis and amongst others are Sisters Longhurst (future Matron of Nevill Hall Hospital), V. Poultney, M. Prosser, D. Harris, Ms. Stevens, Mr. Aubrey, Mr. Pritchard, Mr. Newman, Mr. Pyle, Staff Nurses Hopkins, Meredith and Nurses G. Jaynes, P. Hall, J. Judge, C. Nash, R. Jones, E. Jenkins, M. Morgan, M. Parry, K. Purnell, T. Biggs, G. Collins and E. Chivers. Apologies are extended to those whose names have not been traceable.

48. Nursing is amongst the most noble of professions and here are some local dedicated district nurses to be remembered, looking left to right. Back: Barbara Young, Michelle Zaraski, Vera Jenkins, Joan Methuen, Doreen Griffiths and Kay Williams. Front: Mairwyn Hutchings, Elizabeth Morgan, Annette Caulder and Mirren Martha Lowman.

49. One of Aberbeeg's carnival Queens during the 1950s was Virginia Parfitt who is in the centre of the picture surrounded by her court. Photographed outside the British Legion Hall which was situated opposite the colliery, the gathering includes Jack Clark, Frank Morgan, W.J. Jones (M.D. Webbs), Jane Parry, Moira Thomas, Leonard Newman (Sec. of Webbs), Gaynor Morgan (paying courtesy), Mair Walters and Ernie Bull.

50. This is a group belonging to the 'Prims' Chapel who appear to be dressed in school uniforms of a sort, at an event to raise funds for the chapel in 1950. The pupils are Terry Tucker, M. Thomas, Gwyneth Wilde, Doreen Jones, Clyde Bobbett, Pam Phipps, Doreen Lewis, John Button, Sybil Jones and Joan Galloway.

51. During the 1920s local tennis enthusiasts, together with the support of numerous Aberbeeg residents and business folk constructed their own court, the opening ceremony of which is pictured here. About to cut the tape is Mr. Dixon, a Director of Webbs Brewery accompanied by Mrs. Dixon, sporting a fashionable hat of the day. Also in the picture are Mr. Watkins, Nancy Brown, Ivy Parry, Cyril Pearce, Wyndham James and Edwin Peters.

52. A young Mr. Jack Martindale is seen at the handlebars of his motorcycle accompanied by an unknown pillion passenger outside the premises of W.B. Harrison at Glandwr.

53. There are many residents and familiar faces to be seen here at a VE Day party held at Warm Turn in May 1945. Amongst the crowd are - P. Silcox, B. Jones, Mrs. Edwards, Mrs. Olding, Mrs. Gay, B. Cousins, B. Chapman, Mrs. Nash, Mrs. Arnett, Mrs. Taylor, T. Hoskins, N. Paul, Mrs. Taylor, Alma Tucker, M. Parry, Mrs. Jones, N. Clarke, B. Phelps, Mrs. Tucker, Mrs. Coleman, Mrs. Edwards, Dolly Nash and Mrs. Cunvin.

54. The 1930s was a period of great hardship in the South Wales valleys with unemployment at levels unheard of by today's standards. This was a typical scene at Warm Turn, Aberbeeg when a number of local men, rather than face unending boredom and frustration, decided to construct their own ground for the football and cricket clubs. Thousands of tons of slag were excavated from Warm Turn and the men toiled day and night to provide themselves with their very own sports ground. Some of the workers here are - Back: C. Matthews, Em Boots, Bryn Cousins, W. Baynham, G. Case, J. Bryant, J. Green, I. Davies and W. Heywood. Middle: E. Verrier, R. Elliott and H. Tucker. Front: G. Boots, E. Bell, W. Nash and K. Boots.

55. Players and supporters of Warm Turn Rangers soccer team pose for this picture celebrating a victory some years ago and amongst the crowd are - Stan Bobbett, C. Mapp, George Hall, Eddie Simonds, Ernie Boots, Frank Bell, Vern Griffiths, Jack Mapp, George Bell, Sam Bees, Abe Green, S. Orchard, Eddie Bell, George Radford, Bert Lovell, Tom Bull, Reg Mapp, Will Hayward, R. Boots and Mr. Verrier.

56. To possess one's own motor car in the 1920s was practically unheard of unless of course, you were a local man of some prosperity. Seen here, is Mr. Leslie Webb accompanied by members of his family trying out a new acquisition. Leslie Webb, who lived from 1897 until 1983, was a director of the family-owned brewery, 'Webbs of Aberbeeg'.

57. Three former long-serving members of staff of Webbs brewery are pictured here with a typewriter and duplicating machine, office equipment not seen much these days. The girls are Dorothy Arndell, Morfydd Jones and Pat Carter. Dorothy was secretary to a number of managing directors during her many years of working for Webbs.

58. Two more personalities of the brewery are pictured here when Managing Director Major Sidney Snazell, seen on the right, makes a presentation to Mr. Arthur Kimber who had been with the company since 1939.

59. A carnival float sponsored by Welsh Brewers Limited passes through Abertillery in 1977 and included in the picture are Pat Carter, Morfydd Jones, Ann Warren and Desmond Hale as the Indian chief.

60. Suitably attired, here are some of the girls who worked in the bottling department of Webbs Brewery, namely Marlene Horler, Eileen Holyfield, Beth Pettet, Doris Larkin, Sue Kimber, Doreen Phelps, Olwen Wilkins and Thelma Baker.

61. Three gentlemen take a breather on one of the familiar benches that used to rest outside the Hanbury Hotel. Their names are Bernard Butler, John Pettet and John Purnell.

62. July 1969 saw the celebration of the Investiture of The Prince of Wales, Prince Charles and here is a group of Aberbeeg residents in the party mood which includes - Melvin and Roma Davies, Pedro Nadal, Vern Parfitt, Hazel Robinson, Tom Day, Eileen Taylor, Nesta Griffiths, Joan and Bernard, Shorty Vaughan, Rita and Bryn Cadwallader, Gordon Hill, Sandra Watkins, R. Parfitt, Thelma Lewis, Mrs. Maggs and Morfydd Jones.

63. The young Girl Guides above are Vicky Kimber and Julie Williams who at the age of twelve, when members of the Campaigner Group at Glandwr, had the distinction of winning the coveted Coronet Award for gaining an outstanding number of proficiency awards within the movement.

64. An interior view of the Ivorites from about forty years ago, with members and supporters of Aberbeeg Football Club downing a pint or two. A few names have come to light as follows - Graham Pullinge, Terry Adams, Elwyn Griffiths, Colin Chivers, Mr. Chivers, Dai Cunvin, Mike Allen, Dai Davies, Bob Cousins and Fred Galloway.

65. Carnival time at Warm Turn and whilst the children will now be a little older since this picture was taken, their faces will hopefully recognized by a number of readers.

66. A photograph from the old Aberbeeg School, probably taken during the 1930s. The lady who kindly loaned this picture is Ismerie Hallett, seated in the front row (3rd left) and a granddaughter of William and Rowena Thomas who appear on page 22.

67. Another photograph from the old school, Aberbeeg (since demolished) and the pupils and teacher are, left to right - Back: Alan Shattock, Tony Pearce, Len Jones, Roy Francombe, Gilbert Pyle, Thelma Hambly, Mary Lyn Rees, Sheila Jackson, Ada Thatcher, Albert Evans and Keith Williams. Front: John Thayer, Colin Francombe, Marlene Wilding, Brenda Bennett, Diane Hayward, Gwyneth Newman, ? , M. Parfitt, Marilyn Wall, Sheila Butler, Pat Smith, Philip Lewis, David Larkin, David Lane and Mr. Talbot the headmaster.

68. Class 3 at Ty'r Graig School in 1967 with teacher Mr. Fred Gunter on the far left. The children seen left to right are as follows - Back: Alan Brittain, Joseph Gould, Betty Price, Philip ?, Perry Powell and Patrick Allen. Middle: Alan Curtis, Steven Johnson, Stephen Sutton, Kay Smith, Tony Curtis and Stephen Hewings. Front: Christopher Hill, Robert Deacon, Jayne Morris, Kim Bennett, Lorraine Hunt, John (Robert) Mainwaring and Jeffrey Homer.

69. This picture was taken a year later at Ty'r Graig and accompanying Mr. Gunter this time are - Back: Tommy Tranter, Alan Brittain, Patrick Allen, Glyn Thomas, Stephen Brown, Christopher Assender, Geoffrey Hale and John Mainwaring. Middle: Christopher Hill, Gareth Parsons, Christopher George, Stephen Hewings, Stephen Sutton, Steven Johnson, Philip Atwell, Philip ? and Perry Powell. Front: Jane Morse, Lorraine Hunt, Betty Price, Susan Hunt, Jayne Wilcox, Sharon O'Connell, Alan Crook, Richard Jones and Jeffrey Homer.

70. Here we see a group of girls pictured at Ty'r Graig School and most of the names are known, with apologies to those whom the authors have been unable to trace. Left to right are - Front: Sheila Beech, Pauline Hancock, unknown, Edna Booton. Back: Edna Hopkins, Rita Smith, Dorothy Summers, Lynne Olding, unknown.

71. The year of this school photo from Ty'r Graig is 1960 and maybe a few names will be familiar as follows - Mr. Lewis, Mr. Bevan, M. Evans, D. Bryant, P. Burnett, G. Jones, C. Mahoney, M. Dessman, G. Beckerton, J. Lewis, J. Booton, B. Thacker, G. Beach, N. Wilton, J. Berrow, K. Parfitt, D. Yates, J. Harris, S. Buffin, M. Prichard, L. Watkins, B. Hall, C. Holmes, J. Rees, A. Rees, K. Evans, S. Warren, K. Hallet, D. Smith and J. Brimble.

72. A photograph of some residents of Warm Turn and to be seen are Jim Green, Bill Simmonds, Jack Gough, Ivor Davies and Pearl Baynham.

73. Some cricketers from Warm Turn Cricket Club which was founded in 1921 include Bill Baynham, Abe Green (Sec.), Ivor Davies and Harold Tucker in the front. Harold Tucker, a star cricketer in his day, was also goal-keeper for Penyfan Rangers and a player for Llanhilleth United and Ebbw Vale. Another local cricketer who moved up the ladder of success was Don Skuse who went on to play for Yorkshire.

74. From 1978, comes this picture of the children of Ty'r Graig School after winning the adjudication award for their performance of the play 'Old Zip Coon' at the Gwent Drama Festival held at Blackwood. Unfortunately space does not permit naming all the stars but one up and coming junior actor receiving particular mention on the occasion, was ten year-old Carl Sellick of Brynithel. The proud headmaster of the school at the time was Mr. Ken Phelps.

75. The Primitive Methodist Chapel at Aberbeeg retains history that dates back to the year 1874, when several local miners and their wives took it upon themselves to form a Methodist following of their own. Early worship was conducted in one of the miner's cottages until about 1875, when more spacious accommodation was offered at Powells Colliery Reading Room (later to become Kibby's shop). A few years later, after alterations to Aberbeeg Junction station had been carried out by the Great Western Railway, the society purchased the old wooden-built station house and were now strong enough in numbers to hold Sunday and week-night services, including a Band of Hope. After being incorporated into the extensive Ebbw Vale circuit, the Aberbeeg society saw a period of continued growth in membership. By 1889, there were sufficient funds available to expand even further, and a lease on a plot of land owned by the Hanbury family of Pontypool was taken up. This was an opportunity to secure a permanent site and the first chapel was built there at a cost of £300. In 1905 even this chapel was too small for its congregations, and the decision was taken to construct much larger premises on the same site, an investment costing some £2,000, half of which came from the faithful congregation and their efforts. It is thanks to those efforts by the members, that Aberbeeg Methodist is another one of those places of worship that still survives in a changing world.

76. The Primitive Methodists of Aberbeeg gathered near the former railway station, the period is probably the late 1950s or early 1960s.

77. Some members of the ladies' section of the 'Prims' at the same spot as above, and amongst the group are the Phipps sisters, Barbara and Pam of Warm Turn and Mrs. Warefield of Brewery Terrace.

78. In the 1920s, the membership of the 'Prims' was plentiful as seen by this Whitsun or anniversary walk with more than a hundred adults and children gathered outside the old 'Tin Chapel'.

79. A celebration or anniversary event is in preparation at Glandwr Baptist with a three-tier cake to mark the occasion. Amongst the mostly female party are Eileen Hale, Clarice Hopes, Lilian Dutnall, Mary Applebee (minister's wife), Doreen Walby, Mrs. Jones, Mrs. Rogers, Lavinia, Sheryl Verina Tanner, Jennifer Woods and Grace and Jonathon Applebee.

80. A presentation of cut glass is being made at the Scouts' hut to well-known Scoutmaster Mr. Ted Lewis and his wife, to mark his retirement after long service in the movement.

81. Celebrated Warm Turn musician Ray Walters pictured with two of his saxophones and clarinet, none of which is an easy instrument to learn and play. Ray however was a professional in his field, playing with a number of bands on radio and film.

82. Ted Lewis is seen at the forefront of this group in the local hut which includes Dorothy Meredith, Phyllis Hale and a number of Scouts and Guides.

83. This is Mr. Thomas Willia
Webb Jones who was born in 18`
and reared by his mother i
Aberbeeg. It was this gentlema
who founded the local bus compan
'Jones of Aberbeeg' in 1921, th
blue and yellow-liveried buse
being a familiar sight around th
western valley for some fifty year
The founder died in 1929, leavin
the expanding business to b
continued by his family of wife an
four sons.

84. Mr. Ron Jones is seen here alongside one of his coaches opposite the garage during the 1950s, vehicle number DJ 6581 having been acquired from the St. Helens Corporation, Lancashire in 1954. Ron Jones was the survivor of a family tragedy, when in March 1950, three of his brothers were killed in the Llandow air disaster after returning from the rugby international in Ireland. A total of 83 out of 85 on board were killed, at the time making this the worst accident in civil aviation history.

85. A group of drivers who once worked for the Jones Omnibus Company and in the front are - Tony Verrier, Dennis Simmonds and Garnet Davies. The rest of the crew includes John Horgan, Albert Prior, Herbie Hunt, Archie Hinder, Sam James, Ernie Sweet, Selwyn Hancock and Eric Andrews.

86. One vehicle that former Jones's staff will remember is the 'Presentation Bus' which was used for show and exhibition purposes and amongst the 'followers' seen here are Bob Langdon, Councillor Paddy Byrne, Wyndam Bruten, Stewart Jones, Lyn Rice, Mike (the tyre fitter), Tracy Harries, Ernie Sweet, Sheila Horgan, Archie Hinder, Ron Jones and Ken Parfitt.

87. Some more faces of the staff of Jones's which may be recognizable by readers, the group includes Harold Pitt, Dennis Simmonds, Lawrence Hancock, Albert Prior, Tom Day and Tommy Pitt.

88. A picture probably dating from the early 1960s, shows another two of Jones's buses packed full with local lady residents who unfortunately, are nearly all hidden from view. The lady stood in front of the first coach however is Edith Maud Davies who was chairwoman of Llanhilleth Ladies Labour Party and this photograph was taken during one of their outings. For anyone interested in passenger bus history, the front vehicle was purchased by the Jones company in 1961, using it until 1967 and the second, a 1958 model, Reg. PVJ 700 was purchased from Wye Valley Motors Hereford in 1961 and saw service locally until 1964.

89. An event that was not to be missed in years gone by, was the Christmas party given by the Jones company for their employees and children. Amongst the many here are, Back - Gary Jones, Ken Parfitt, Jim Lewis, June Parfitt and Jeanette Jones. Middle - David Lewis, Elwyn Lewis, Norman Lewis and Janet Phipps. Adults on the left include Georgina Jones, Elaine Jones, Dorothy Jones and Mary Jones. In the front are Mike Jones, Gordon Griffiths and Joan Griffiths.

90. A Bedford coach is parked outside the Jones depot, a vehicle that was originally built in 1950 but not purchased by the company until 1960. By the late 1960s, smaller bus operators were being integrated with the National Bus Company and the Aberbeeg business and service routes, became part of the Red and White group.

91. This photograph from the 1960s is of Des Warren although the pseudonym 'Sarge' will be more familiar to anyone who has travelled on local transport. Des spent a lifetime 'on the buses', having started as a conductor with Jones's after demob from the Army with the rank of sergeant in 1947, and it was this event that led to his everlasting nickname.

There were no uniforms available to Jones's staff in the years following the war, and Des was obliged to dye his military clothing navy blue. Unfortunately his sergeant's stripes left a permanent mark on the jacket, which could not be disguised. Consequently his fellow workmates were quick to spot this and hence 'Sarge' of the buses was born!

92. Whilst the street is dominated by a 'walk' by members of the Prims, there are two buildings in the background to be remembered that have since changed somewhat. The Post Office is nowadays a private dwelling and the Police Station, next door, has been converted into flats.

93. A local personality, who will not be easily recognized here, after winning the May Queen competition at Abertillery in 1938, but the name will be more familiar. The lady is Elizabeth (Pat) Longhurst, who began her long and distinguished nursing career at Aberbeeg Hospital in 1948, graduating to nursing sister on the gynaecological ward. In 1955 Miss Longhurst transferred to the old Nevill Hall Hospital in Abergavenny as Matron, and subsequently achieved the accolade of being appointed the first Matron of the new and prestigious Nevill Hall which opened in 1969.

94. More local personalities are pictured here in about 1959-60 as members of the Potters Club Ladies Darts Team. Seen left to right, proudly displaying a trophy are Sal Stonuary, Betty Buffin, Mrs. G. Hopes, Joan Wilkins and Janet Mountjoy.

95. Aberbeeg railwayman Bob Fowler is pictured here in the cab of his diesel locomotive. As with Des Warren, mentioned earlier, Bob also devoted his life to public transport, having worked on the railways in days of steam and diesel from the age of fourteen for a staggering forty-eight years. Passing away in 1998, Bob will also be remembered for his services to local rugby, becoming President of Aberbeeg Club after retirement.

96. An Aberbeeg 'Sevens' side with a young mascot and a display of trophies are seen on the field during the 1959-60 season. Just a few names have been recalled from the back row - Gilbert Lovell, B. Woodland and Councillor Clarke. In the front the young lad is Dafydd Lloyd and just behind him on the right is his father Ron Lloyd.

97. A souvenir photograph of Aberbeeg R.F.C. in 1970-71 and starting from the left, back row are - B. Woodland, D. Adams, D. Evans, T. Cox, K. Miles, C. Hutchings, B. Butler, E. Saunders, K. Hall, J. Edmunds, B. Fowler, L. Watkins, V. Parfitt, L. Browne, G. Roles, J.R. Clarke, W. Barker, W. Chivers, J. Harris and C. Parfitt.

98. Waiting on the Square (when there was one) in Aberbeeg, are members of the R.F.C. awaiting transport to begin a tour of the USA. The gentleman on the left holding the ball, is Ron Turner, a well-known character and Aberbeeg player for many years and now in his nineties.

99. Pictured in the grounds of Brondeg House are these rugby players who were winners of the Western Valley League in the 1919-20 season. They are, left to right, Back row: T. Thomas (Trainer), C. Wilde, W. Beams, G. King, W. Griffiths, T. David, Councillor J. Jones, I. Saunders. W. Davies, L. Richards, B. Fox, A. Powell, F. Thatcher, H. Lewis, W.R. Broome (Secretary). Middle Row: T. Thomas, A. Davies, B. Taylor, O. Richards, T. Davies, R. Powell and L. Davies. Front row: I. Weybourne, R. Saunders, J. Parfitt (Vice Captain), S. Saunders (Captain), G. Griffiths, I. Bolt, W. Lewis and F. Grail.

100. The concluding photograph in this chapter is of another Aberbeeg 'Fifteen' and includes Gerald Boucher, Basil Mills, Bob Fowler, Ron Lloyd and Alan Wanklyn.

CHAPTER 3

Views of Llanhilleth

101. The English Baptist Church of Llanhilleth opened in 1896 with seating for 600 worshippers. Now demolished, residents may still remember its location which was close to the present-day Llanhilleth Rugby Club.

102. St. Illtyd's Church Llanhilleth which stands some 370 metres above sea level, is one of Gwent's oldest buildings. Having been substantially altered and rebuilt in the ninth century and then in the late twelfth century by a group of Cistercian monks, the church can claim history dating back to the fifth century; the first building being of wooden construction.

Llanhilleth or 'Llanilltyd', a parish in the manor of Wentsland and Bryngwyn, was until 1535, the property of Llantarnam Abbey and the church served as the Parish Church until 1910, prior to the opening of Christ Church at Aberbeeg. Numerous ancient relics have survived, such as an eighth century font and bells cast in 1615 and 1767, the latter commemorating a visit to Llanhilleth by Methodist leader, John Wesley. By the year 1957 however, the church was forced to close, mainly due to opencast mining in the area which continued for a further five years. During this time, the building fell into sad decay and was totally abandoned until the Church of Wales passed it on to private ownership in 1984.

Suddenly the church's historical value was appreciated and the Borough Council successfully applied for a compulsory purchase order. A £130,000 renovation scheme was launched and after a lengthy period of toil and effort, the work was completed in 1993, the site becoming a popular tourist spot, attracting visitors from various parts of the globe.

The picture above will be of particular interest if studied carefully. To the right of the tree is an apparition of a mysterious robed gentleman, an unexpected visitor when the film was developed. Tales of such apparitions are plentiful however, one reason being attributed to the unrest of a lady by the name of Joan White, who was burned to death as a local witch in ancient times!

103. The old church that once stood in the grounds of Brynithel cemetery, it holding services there until the 1940s. The building later suffered at the hands of land subsidence and was eventually demolished in the 1980s. This picture is from about 1908, and some typical charges administered by Abertillery Council in dealing with the departed at the time were as follows - interment of a pauper for 28 pence, a common grave for a parishioner at 63 pence and a large family vault for £6.25. On all such funeral occasions, the bell could be tolled as an optional extra for five pence an hour.

104. From about ninety years ago comes this view of the rear of the Royal Oak public house and adjacent houses. Abandoned and then falling into a state of poor repair, the houses made national news headlines in 1999 and 2000, when they were eventually sold at a 'knock-down price' for restoration and development. In the left foreground can be seen the former signal box alongside the railway lines.

105. A scene from early days before the road surfaces had received proper attention in about 1910. Hafod-Arthen is on the left, Blaencuffin Road on the right and in the background is Troy Road.

106. A wide-sweeping outlook that captures some of Llanhilleth's landmarks. Such buildings to be observed include The Playhouse, Top Hotel, Railway Station and The Institute.

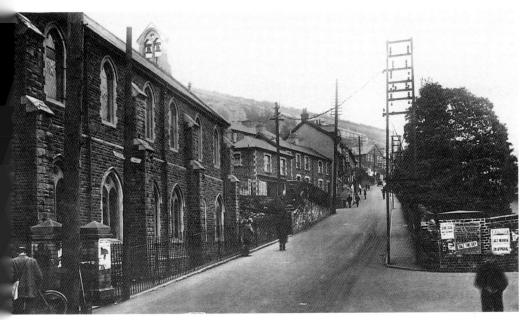

107. A view looking up the hill during the 1920s with two places of worship from differing denominations in sight. On the upper left is the Wesleyan Methodist Chapel and nearest the camera is St. Mark's Church. St. Mark's was built in 1898, typically constructed of stone in the Gothic style with a distinctive two-bell cote as seen on the roof. The original provision was for a congregation of almost 400 and whilst this has diminished considerably, St. Mark's still survives in the town.

108. A general view from the mountainside looking towards Llanhilleth that shows amongst other things the development of Brynithel, whilst below are Ty'r Graig School and Glandwr Chapel.

109. Llanhilleth Station in about 1906 and the houses of Railway Street have not long been built; those streets yet to be constructed are Partridge Road and Caefelin Street. Originally owned by the Monmouthshire Railway and Canal Company, the railway line through Llanhilleth was opened in the early 1850s, providing new and swift transport of goods and passengers down the valley to Newport. The facilities at Llanhilleth Station improved considerably when The Great Western Railway took over in 1880. As already mentioned in the text, the

110. Looking down the hill during the early years of the twentieth century and the street at the time is littered with shops. The horse and cart, the only sign of traffic, is stood approximately outside the post office, which at the time was in the hands of Mr. James Mead who also owned a busy grocery shop.

111./112. Two photographs that show a number of places of interest in the district, some have since been demolished and some still remain. Above are St. David's Catholic Church, Baptist Chapel, Walpole Hotel and Gorman's. In the lower picture are the fields, the rear of the Central Hotel, Brynhfryd School and the Belle Vue Club.

113. A view that was taken from near the Institute many years ago. The house in the lower foreground is Llanhilleth House, a former residence, amongst others, of William Webb founder of Aberbeeg's brewery. In later years it was used as housing for the colliery managers before eventually being knocked down to make way for the Grace Pope complex.

114. Facing in a northerly direction in the late 1940s, and there are another two prominent buildings in view. Bottom left is the Central Hotel, just one of a number of former hotels in Llanhilleth and on the near right, is a long-closed branch of Barclays Bank. There were two banks serving the town in its heyday, the other being the London Joint City and Midland, in Commercial Road. These days the nearest banks are probably in Abertillery.

115. This is how many local residents will best remember the Central Hotel, in days when it was a popular venue for many a social function. Designed by Cardiff architect Mr. Telford Evans, it was built in 1905 in response to a rapidly expanding community and cost a huge amount for the period, some £6,000. The first recorded landlord was Mr. Albert Simmonds.

116. Llanhilleth Workmen's Institute, a centre for entertainment and social gatherings for almost a century. Funded by colliery owners Partridge Jones, and the miners themselves, the first stone was laid in October 1904 and the official opening by Welsh cross-country champion, Tom Arthur took place in May 1906. The building housed an indoor swimming pool, reading room, billiard hall and a large concert hall which also served as a cinema. At one time even the County Magistrates performed their duties on the premises. The Institute has changed somewhat nowadays, the pool having been covered over and now home to the local library with the billiard hall presently occupied by a doctor's surgery. The main hall however does retain some of its original intentions as a popular dance hall and use as a function room.

117. Photographed in the 1950s or 1960s, this is how the backs of housing in the area known locally as 'The Fields', looked in those days. The view is looking north towards Aberbeeg.

118. Another view well-illustrating the industrial housing of Llanhilleth, this time looking south with the Miners' Institute in the distance. The scene is during the days when there was dust, dirt and grime discharging from the colliery and smoke from the coal fires; today's readers can imagine the problems endured by local housewives in keeping their washing clean as seen on the lines here.

119. This is an early view taken from the Christchurch area that shows a rather remote house close to the railway line. The second field to the south side of the house is Joby Jaynes's field, the first home of Llanhilleth Cricket Club.

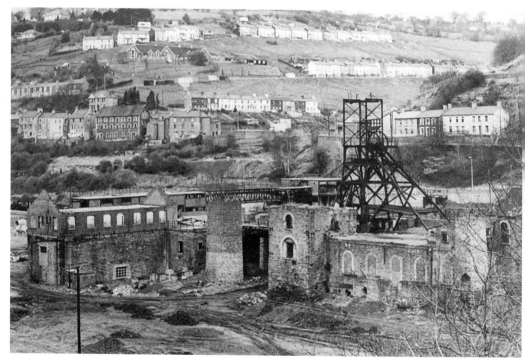

120. A scene of dereliction at the former Llanhilleth colliery in the 1970s. Virtually every colliery has experienced a serious accident in its lifetime, but one at Llanhilleth in March 1905 was recorded as 'a most unusual event'. Seven men were badly injured, one subsequently dying, in what was thought to be an explosion - the usual cause. The official report however disclosed that there was no such explosion or evidence of gas to cause it. The findings were, that a fall had taken place causing a huge compression of air which swept the men several yards through the air as if hit by a mighty cannonball. The deceased was Mr. Dennis Carrol of Lancaster Street, Six Bells.

121. A look down the hill in Commercial Street during the 1920s is a reminder of just how steep this part of Llanhilleth really is. There are two early motor vehicles in sight and in those days of small and inefficient engines, they would have found this hill to be a testing experience. Earlier horse-drawn traffic would have found it a torment.

122. High Street Llanhilleth during the 1920s was quite a busy shopping centre with well over twenty traders of all description in business. Immediately on the right is Morris's the tobacconist and confectioner, next door to the local police station which was built in 1898. At the time of this photograph, Sergeant Frederick Campbell was in charge, assisted by four constables. In the background is the Playhouse, a source of cinema and choral entertainment for about sixty years and since demolished.

123. Llanhilleth Collieries, of which the first shaft was sunk in the year 1870, and during the peak years of coal production at the outbreak of war in 1914 some 1900 men were employed here.

124. An extended view of Hafodarthen Road from the beginning of the twentieth century, when the road was in an undeveloped state and there was just one gas lamp to illuminate the whole street.

125. Another look at High Street, this time facing in a southerly direction in 1908. Two shops on the immediate left are the drapery department of the Co-op and next door is James Bartlett the grocer. As stated previously, there was a wide variety of shops in High Street at the time, including a music warehouse, a plumber, a fried fish dealer and two artificial teeth-makers by the name of Harvey Roots and George Nightingal.

126./127. Two pictures of Hafod-y-coed, the upper, from about 1905 and the lower some twenty years later, this picture providing a view of Horseshoe Bend.

128./129. The Llanhilleth branch of the Blaina Industrial Co operative Society was once the largest store in the town employing nearly thirty staff and selling anything from a joint of meat to a pair of shoes. Mr William Oriel was the branch manager when these pictures were taken in about 1915.

130. A stationary pannier tank engine and guard's van are seen on the once-busy railway tracks at Llanhilleth. In the background is the bridge leading down to the fields from Commercial Road with the houses of Brynithel on the skyline.

131. An ancient photograph that was taken near Horseshoe Bend and the prominent building in the background is the old school. In front of the school are the houses of Hillside Terrace, some of Llanhilleth's earliest residences which were built here in 1875.

132. Stood outside their shop in Commercial Road are members of the Crockett family, the proprietor being Mr. George Crockett. This picture was taken when the shop was a general store, but in previous years the business was run as 'Refreshment Rooms'.

133./134. There must be some readers who will remember Hunt's leather goods shop in Commercial Road (the premises now a gift and flower shop and adjacent mini market). The founder was Abraham Hunt, who was born in Chippenham in 1884 and after serving the necessary apprenticeship, set up his own business in 1909; at the time his advertisements interestingly read as a saddler, collar maker, fancy leather goods dealer with special attention given to colliery requisites. As trade flourished he was joined by his three brothers, acquiring an additional shop in Llanhilleth and opening new premises in Blackwood shortly before World War One. In the upper picture founder Abraham is seen outside the original Llanhilleth store and below, brother George is stood outside the expanded business next door.

135. A view of the colliery looking in a southerly direction. Originally sunk by Walter Powell, the undertaking was soon taken over by Partridge Jones and Company until nationalization. There were limited coal workings here as far back as 1802 but when the new shaft was sunk the...

136. The collieries are seen in full swing here during the late 1920s. The district was rich in coal with four seams being worked to exhaustion, the average yearly output in the heydays often exceeding 200,000 tons. Those heydays however, together with many valuable jobs, came to an end when Llanhilleth Colliery finally closed in March 1969.

137. Regents Place as seen here is a typical example of difficult, but efficient house-building at the turn of the last century. The rows of houses were cut deep into the mountainside, often with retaining walls up to five metres high. The upper row has been built in a semi-detached fashion and the lower in blocks of eight.

138. A photograph taken from on high, that overlooks the long platforms of Llanhilleth station. The railway tracks heading down the valley continued in two directions, the next stop on the main line being Crumlin Low Level. There was also a single branch line which climbed the steep gradient towards Swffryd and on to the halt at Hafodyrynys. The junction of these two lines was just north of the Royal Oak houses and although the track was never used for official public transport, it remained open until 1961 carrying Western Valley workers to the Ordnance factory at Glascoed.

139. An unusual photograph that was taken from the valley's most famous landmark until the 1960s, Crumlin Viaduct. The view is looking north towards Llanhilleth, the housing on the right still being known as Upper and Lower Viaduct Terrace. On the left are the local colliery workings, with the main railway lines in the centre which now form the route of the new road.

140. Just a mile or two down the road from Llanhilleth at Crumlin, stood an important brewery, just like Webbs of Aberbeeg, supplying many of the valley's public houses - the company of D.F. Prichard Ltd. This is their early 1900's steam wagon, often seen delivering beers to two of their Llanhilleth customers, The Royal Oak and Central Hotel.

141. In the centre of this photograph from the 1930s is Brynhyfryd School and the large house to the left, is the local doctor's residence, subsequently converted into the Belle Vue Club. A few statistics from the period confirm that the town was once a substantial place in which to live, with an area of 2,000 acres of land and a civil parish population of more than 10,000.

142. The final picture in this chapter is exceptionally early, probably dating from around 1904. This is evidenced by the fact that the Institute has not yet been constructed and the houses of Meadow Street are nearing completion.

CHAPTER 4

Llanhilleth, Brynithel People & Events

143. A carnival float makes its way down Meadow Street with the Institute in the background. Whilst the authors have no names to offer, the girls are portraying 'The TV Toppers', and some readers may well remember the original group performing on television during the 1950s and '60s, together with the Billy Cotton Band.

144. Another carnival group from the 1950s and the grass-skirted entrants include - Standing: Mrs. Davies, Elsie Jones and Sheila Beech who are accompanied at the back by Alf Ward and Jim Burton. Seated: Joan Peck, Ivy Burton, Tilly Perrett, Bronwyn Davies, Nel Burton, Betty Phelps, Doreen Williams and Becky Williams. Foreground: Ruby Phelps and Stan Jones.

145. Never before, or since, have such large crowds been seen congregated outside the Central Hotel, listening to a speech given by a gentleman stood on a platform on the left. Judging by the flags and bunting, the occasion is thought to be either the proclamation of King George V in 1910 or perhaps the celebration of the end of the war in November 1918.

146. Members of The Belle Vue Club pose for a photograph outside their hotel, during an excursion to that favourite resort Blackpool, probably during the late 1950s. Amongst the crowd are Mr. and Mrs. Phelps, W. Woodland, F. Box, Mr. and Mrs. G. Pound, Mrs. Bryant, B. Legge, Laura Carter, Alice Thomas, Betty Williams, Mrs. Harris, Brenda Nicholls, Mrs. Lewis, Mrs. Vaughan, Liz Rogers, Mrs. Brimble, Mrs. Dentry and four members of the Chivers family.

147. The three gentlemen above are pictured backstage at Llanhilleth Institute where they were responsible for the technicalities of lighting and stage-management during the days of regular performances held there. Pictured left to right may be seen Derek Parsons, Len Carpenter and Jack Parsons.

148. This photograph was taken in front of the screen at that other one-time venue for good entertainment - The Playhouse. Apparently in the process of making a speech is the well-known Doctor Scanlon and behind him are Mr. Bosher, Mr. L. Carpenter, Bill Jones, Stan Butler and Bill Fossey.

The Workmen's Institute - Llanhilleth

(By kind permission of the Institute Committee)

FOR FIVE NIGHTS
Tuesday, April 21st to Saturday April 25th, 1959

The Illtyd Amateur Operatic Society
CELEBRATES ITS

22nd Presentation of Operetta
WITH

The Gipsy Princess

a new version of Emmerich Kalman's famous operetta

By LEO STEIN and BELA JENBACH

Music adapted and arranged by RONALD HANMER

Lyrics by PHIL PARK and CONRAD CARTER

By arrangement with N.O.D.A
on behalf of JOSEF WEINBERGER Ltd.

Stage production under the sole direction of

Jack and Melba Wells

Musical Director: MR. MARTIN BUDD, A.T.C.L.

Accompanist : MISS ELAINE HUMPHRIES

Orchestra under the leadership of
MR. HAYDN BOND.

FLASHBACK

Do you remember ?
The Illtyd Operatic Society presented
"San Marino" at the Llanhilleth
Workmen's Institute in 1936 and the
cast was as follows :-

PABLO	MR. SID PURKISS
DICKY	MR. A. BABER
1ST PORTER	MR. E. REED
2ND PORTER	MR. C. MORGAN
ROSITA	MRS. E. LANE
PEPITA	MISS I. SYMONDS
CHIQUITA	MRS. J. WILCOX
DOLORES	MISS M. LEWIS
GENERAL MARTINEZ	MR. C. EVANS
GASPAR	MR. JOE WILCOX
CARLOS SANTEZ	MR. JACK WILCOX
LUIS	MR. A. PARRY
LOLA	MRS. W. HARRIS
HIRAM	MR. G. BAKER
ANNABEL	MISS B. BLACKMORE
RIQUETTE	MISS V. EDMUNDS

149. There is a total of almost fifty performers and supporters seen in this early picture from the St. Illtyd Amateur Operatic Society. The Society was formed in 1919, when a party of seven enthusiasts led by Mr. David Edwards, who happened to live near St. Illtyd's Church, formed a group calling themselves The Illtyd Glee Singers. Enormous success followed, thanks to the support of a number of local talented artistes and by 1926, the Society had embarked on their first full operatic production.

150./151. Two scenes from the Society's performance of 'A Country Girl' at the Institute in 1952 and most of the stars have been identified. Back: Muriel Carter, Phyllis Lewis, Mrs. Angel, May Dayton, Basil ?, Alma Bowen, Marjorie Collett, Mrs. Jones and Gladys Vernon. Front: Kitty Carter, Noreen Inwood and Laura Lewis.

152. Some costumed ladies and a priest belonging to the Society cast are seen during the 1930s and a few names have come to light as follows - Iris Simmonds, Olwen Holmes (1st and 2nd from the left), Mr. Jesse Carter and Mrs. Carter (4th and 5th from the left).

153. Supporters would relish any new show performed by Society knowing that attendances would be to the full. Here is the cast of the musical 'The Arcadians', which played to a packed house for a week in the Workmen's Institute in March 1954 and among the many are - Hughie Carter, Ernest Pratley, Ernest Bull, Towy Berrow, Eric Blackford, Gwen Pope, Mrs. Edwards, Mrs. Angel, Marjorie Collett, Mrs. Jones, Phyllis Neads, Jack Wanklyn, George and May Dayton, Gladys Vernon, Heather Flook, Elma Bowen and Iris Clark.

154. Here is a collection of photographs of just a few of the many ladies and gentlemen who did so much to support the Society in years gone by.

Jack Wells

Melba Wells

Martin Budd

Elaine Humphries

A warm welcome for our chief citizen

Councillor W. H. Jones, J.P. a strong supporter of the Society and President of Llanhilleth Workmen's Institute, will pay an official visit, as Abertillery's chief citizen, on Thursday evening.

Councillor W.H. Jones, J.P.

Jack Wanklyn

Gwenllian Price

Mr. Towy Berrow

Mr. Merlyn Neads

Mr. J. Glyn Edwards

Mrs. Catherine Carter

155. On the far right is Mrs. Phyllis Neads of Llanhilleth who is sharing some of her talent with some Operatic Society students under instruction. The venue is Ebbw Vale college in 1959 and the production is 'The Gypsy Baron' with Phyllis playing Cizipra.

156. Some local personalities are seen here during a presentation and a few names to be remembered are - Mr. and Mrs. Thomas of Aberbeeg, Elaine Humphries, Towy Berrow, Merlyn Neads, Glyn Edwards (Manager of Barclays Bank) and Councillor W.H. Jones J.P.

157. Many local girls are to be seen here as members of the Cwmbran Ladies Hockey Club who were Welsh Champions in 1986. They are, back: April Jeffries (Llanhilleth), Glynis Jones, Helen Thomas, Paula James (Cwm), Anne Marie Davies (Brynmawr), Margaret Birchmore (Coach, Llanhilleth), Susan Waters (Abertillery), Julie Carpenter (Newbridge), Margaret Donald and Hazel Webley (Nantyglo). Front: Catherine Griffiths, Barbara Corne, Margaret Thomas (Abertillery), Shoona Franks (Captain), Christine Hicks (Brynmawr), Pat Boulter and Jane Webb.

Coach Margaret Birchmore has much to be proud of during her long association with ladies' hockey. She began playing in 1943 whilst attending Newbridge Grammar School and embarked on a sporting career that lasted for fifty years until her final retirement in 1993. After leaving school she continued to play at college in Swansea, subsequently returning to a teaching appointment in Brynmawr Grammar and Secondary schools. As hockey became quite popular in the 1960s, with more facilities being provided by the authorities, Margaret joined Newport Athletic Club ladies hockey section intent on developing her skills. Unfortunately a serious road accident brought a swift end to her playing aspirations, but not the passion for the game. It was at this point that she graduated to an International umpire and soon saw coaching as being a favoured progression, one that was to be recognized and appreciated far and wide.

The list of achievements thereafter is long and commendable. The Newport Athletic's Ladies Hockey Club was to become the Cwmbran Club and coaching was provided for them by Margaret. She soon followed this with coaching for the Monmouthshire and South Wales teams (junior and senior), then the accolade of Internationals; firstly with Wales schoolgirls, Wales under 21 and finally in 1973 Wales itself. In 1975 Wales, seeded ninth in the world reached the final of the World Cup in Edinburgh, some proud moments for the girls and their coach. Many towns worldwide have taken part in the game of hockey over the years; the Cwmbran Club went on to win the Welsh Cup and in 1987, the European Cup in Katowice, Poland. Any young girl showing promise in the sport was taken under Margaret Birchmore's wing and coached to the highest of standards. Amongst the many achievers over the years were included, three full Welsh caps - Margaret Snook (Thomas), Judith Nelder (Leigh) and Susan Waters. April Jeffries was one to gain a Schoolgirl Cap and many more of Margaret's protégés were to play for Cwmbran and Monmouthshire.

158. This is a gathering of members of the Co-operative Trade and Provident Movement whilst parading up High Street. The banner carries the title Bristol West of England and South Wales but there are a number of local men to be seen here in the year 1912 including Llew Elliott, Albert Box, Tom Lewis, Windsor Davies, Edgar Rogers and a Mr. W. Williams of Llanharan.

159. Just one of the many chapel marches that were a regular occurrence in years gone by, this one being in Commercial Road in about 1910. In the background a number of old shops are to be seen such as William Holmes a confectioner and café owner, Buchan Brothers the drapers, Benjamin Jelly a hairdresser and further down, Woodleys the butchers.

160. The lady and gentleman on the left are Samuel and Elizabeth Hill pictured at their mountainside home 'Travellers Rest', high on the hills past St. Illtyd's. Elizabeth Hill was perpetually known to everyone as 'Granny Hill' and was a remarkable woman during her lifetime, which ended in 1939 at the grand old age of 99. She would be seen every week without fail, trekking the arduous route from Travellers Rest to Six Bells Post Office and back to collect her old age pension; a feat she carried out until ninety years of age.

161. Some more members of the Hill family are seen here near TyDaffyd Farm in the area known as Travellers Rest. The name Travellers Rest originates from an ancient inn that once stood nearby, serving mountain walkers and travellers and the farm was situated on top of the hillside overlooking Six Bells. The family seen here consists of Evan Hill (son of Grannie), wife Emily and daughters Bessie, Gwyneth and Myfanwy who are also accompanied by their friend Noreen Geary. Evan Hill was also known to be the owner of a small house-coal level at Travellers Rest for some years.

162. A party of Llanhilleth gentlemen are pictured whilst on holiday in Blackpool probably in the late 1950s or early '60s. The line-up is, left to right - Trevor Jones, Leonard Chivers, Trevor Creed, Brian Hurle (?), Derek Kimber, Terry Thomas and Gwyn Thomas.

163. A whole coach-load of Llanhilleth holidaymakers are seen outside their hotel here in Blackpool in August 1953, on a trip organised by Jim Lewis. The faces will be familiar but regettably are too numerous to mention.

164. Members of Llanhilleth Jazz Band in some fancy dress during the early 1950s at the pit-head baths. Starting at the top, many names are known, such as - Brian Jones, Reg Attwell, Richard Rice, Lenny Minchin, Terry Meek, Lawrence Christie, Mr. Shapcott, Leonard Perrot, Bryn Williams, Mr. George, Ronnie Webber (stood on the wall), Boyo Phillips, I. Webber, Trevor Jones, Leonard Jones, Alan Creese, Brian Andrews, Brian Buffin, Graham Davies, Mr. Lane, Derek Kimber, Lawrence Lane, Lawrence Insley, Mr. Saunders, Mr. Webber (drummer), Mr. T. Jones, Jack Watkins and Derek Jones (holding the baton).

165. Girls belonging to the Rachel Simkins Tap Dance Troupe pose for a photograph in 1951 and from right to left starting at the back are - Pat Blanchard, Gladys Lewis, Phyllis Carter, Pat Corbett(?), Glenys Creese and Margaret Brimble.

166. The Belle Vue Club was originally a private house before being converted into a club under a few different names. The last resident was Mr. Stanfield who had interests in Marine Colliery, Cwm. Often still referred to as Stanfield House, it was to become the Ex Servicemen's Club, British Legion and now the Belle Vue. In this photograph from Coronation Day, June 2nd 1953, Hannah Morgan is surrounded by some of her customers including Joe Coombes, Eddie Donald, Billy Buffin, Jimmy Young and Billy Woodward.

167. An event no longer celebrated in Llanhilleth is the Colliery Dinner and a few guests seen here at the table are Merlyn and Phylis Neads with Mr. Johnson (manager) and his wife.

THE LLANHILLETH RELIEF FUND, 1926.

List of Subscriptions and Donations Received.
(ARRANGED UNDER DISTRICTS.)

"A" ABERBEEG.

	£	s.	d.
Burgess, W. E.	7	10	0
Collings, H.	1	5	0
Davies, Dr. T. Ashton ...	1	1	0
Dixon, Councillor J. ...	6	0	0
Edmunds, H.		8	0
Felix, Rev. D.	23	0	0
Field, W. E.		10	6
Glandwr Sunday School	1	0	0
Jones, F.	1	0	0
Rowland, J. E.		10	6
South Wales Miners' Federation ...		10	0
Staff Contributions :—			
Aberbeeg Colliery	4	4	6
Messrs. W. Thomas & Sons ...	4	0	0
Thomas, Lionel	6	15	0
Tovey, J.	1	10	0
Webb's (Aberbeeg) Limited ...	95	0	0
Webb, W. E. K.	2	2	0
Workmen's Club and Institute Limited	25	4	0
	£181	**10**	**6**

———0———

"C" LLANHILLETH.

	£	s.	d.
Buchan, A. H.	1	5	0
Carpanini, F.		7	6
Carter, J.	2	0	0
Crotty, L. M.		17	0
Davies, Mrs.		8	0
Dixon, P.		2	0
Downs, Miss R.	1	15	0
Flook, G.		16	0
Gorman, Alderman M. ...	16	0	0
Griffiths, T. (M.E.) ...	4	15	0
Hallett, W.	1	5	0
Harper, W.	5	15	0
Hewett, T.	8	2	6
Holmes, W. J.		17	6
Hopkins, C. G.		7	6
Horseman, G.	1	5	0
Jacklyn, H.		12	6
Jones, W.	3	2	6
Jones, Mrs. A.		5	0
Levy, I.	5	4	0
Lewis, H.	21	0	0
Marks, I.	4	7	6
Mead, J.		2	6
Paget, A.	1	8	0
Rawlinson, F.		10	0
Roskyn, B.	3	2	6
Sheldrake, W.	10	0	0
Smart, J.	5	0	0
Staff Contributions—			
Barclays Bank, Limited ...	2	5	0
Mr. Hall's shop	1	4	0
India & China Tea Company ...	1	5	0
Llanhilleth Colliery ...	124	10	0
Workmen's Institute ...	7	19	0
Taylor, P.	3	10	0
Thayer, Miss B.		4	0
Thomas, Mr.		15	0
Wall, F.		5	0
Workmen's Institute ...	180	0	0
	£367	**9**	**6**

"B" ABERTILLERY & SIX BELLS.

	£	s.	d.
Abertillery & District Association of the National Union of Teachers (Aberbeeg and Llanhilleth ...	54	3	6
Arrail Griffin Medical Aid & Hospital Fund, Six Bells ...	15	1	0
Christian Endeavour Convention ...	4	0	0
Dagger, G. ...		2	6
National Association of Local Government Officials (Abertillery Branch)	28	10	3
Order of the Hospital of St. John of Jerusalem	4	0	0
South Wales Miners' Federation ...	27	11	9
	£123	**8**	**11**

"D" VARIOUS OTHER PLACES.

		£	s.	d.
Dix, H. ...	Cwm	5	5	0
Ford & Branch, Limited,	Gloucester	1	0	0
Mellos, H. W. ...	Bath	1	0	0
Amalgamated Society of Woodworkers,	Newbridge		12	6
Pegler's Stores, Limited,	Newport	1	1	0
Phillips, Dr. Marion ...	London	10	0	0
Tolson, H. H. ...	Newport	5	0	0
Webb, Mrs. M. A. ...	Addlestone	31	10	0
		£55	**8**	**6**

168. The effects of the Miners and General Strikes of 1926 brought devastating hardship to communities nationwide, levels of which, even exceeded the experiences in the 1984 mining dispute. Whilst the T.U.C. called off the General Strike after nine days, the miners fought on, a war of attrition developing between the government, the coal owners and the miners for another seven months. Seen above is a list of mostly local sympathizers who helped families 'stay afloat' at the time, and at the end of it all, a total of 40,626 meals had been provided for the needy of the district.

169./170. Both of these pictures depict some of Mr. John Carter's charabanc outings for some local ladies and their children in the 1920s. Above the trippers are at Barry Island (as the speed of these vehicles was little more than 20 mph, the journey would not have been too comfortable) and below, a larger and more modern vehicle is seen outside the Hafodyrynys Hotel 'ready for the off'.

171. A parade by members of the Presbyterian Sunday School along High Street possibly during the 1930s. As the street is quite festooned with flags and decorations, the period could well be the Silver Jubilee celebrations of 1935.

172. A popular grocery shop in Commercial Road Llanhilleth that served the public long before the arrival of supermarkets was that known as the India and China Tea. This picture from 1959 shows manager Mr. Alf Jones with his assistants Mary Morgan and Norma Slocombe. The customer in front of the counter is Mrs. Trimm.

173. On the far left is Doctor John Frost who is pictured with some of his patients, all of whom constitute five generations of one family. In the centre is Mrs. Mary Hayes, accompanied by her daughter Ruth, grandson Bill Butler, great grandson Jack Butler and a baby great great granddaughter Jennifer Butler.

174. These local lads are ready to return to Llanhilleth after a working holiday pea-picking in Kent during the 1950s. Most of them appear to be pipe-smokers and left to right are Derek Jones, Chalky Owen, Billy Woodward, Phil Bevan, Billy Mitchell, Bryn Harwood, Niblo Davies and Joe Phelps.

175./176. Over the railway bridge and Commercial Road are the settings for members of the independent faiths to march in song during the 1920s and 1950s. As non-conformism worship made its presence felt in the valley in the eighteenth century, and in the absence of official places of prayer, it fell upon dedicated individuals to rally to the cause. One such person was a lady Nest Shon Prosser, who opened up her cottage on Llanhilleth's mountainside as the towns first 'preaching centre'. For the Baptists of Llanhilleth, their mentor was Thomas Griffiths of Abertillery who did so much to further their beliefs at the end of the nineteenth century.

177. About to cross the winning line is Llanhilleth-born Colin Weaver who was a sprinting legend in his day. Starting at the age of just nine years, he later turned to professional running, a decision that prevented him from possible Olympic consideration. At the height of his career in the 1930s, the media even compared him to the immortal Jesse Owens and his achievements would be quite familiar in cinema newsreels of the period. His enthusiasm for sport continued long after retirement including the training of Welsh athlete Gareth Edwards and rugby player Paul Ring. Colin Weaver passed away in the year 2000 at a respectable age of 86.

178. Some readers of this book may well remember a very popular factual TV series during the 1970s *'Edward and Mrs. Simpson'* portraying the love affair between the King of England, Edward VIII and American divorcee Mrs. Wallis Simpson. The affair rocked the Government, Nation and Royal Family, leading to the unprecedented abdication of a ruling monarch in 1936. As the King had himself visited the district earlier in 1936, it was perhaps appropriate that Llanhilleth be chosen as a site for part of the filming. Edward was played by star Edward Fox who is seen here with other members of the cast in Meadow Street in 1976.

179. Some members of the local community also made an appearance and seen here are Shad Davies, Joe Phelps, Edward Fox (dressed in bowler hat and looking uncanningly like the real king), Mr. Woodward (Bogsy) and Teddy Nicholls.

180. Among the many inhabitants lining Meadow Street, as cheering crowds on the film set were Eva Cadwell, Phylis Neads, Rhys Protheroe and Winnie Dyer. During the four-day filming session, the Institute was used as the TV company's headquarters with a number of locals providing some 1930s traditional costume.

181. Llanhilleth R.F.C. celebrated its centenary in 1998 and this photograph marks the event. Seated left to right are - Robert Pritchard, Merlyn Neads, Russell Connelly, Mervyn Crees, Roger Adison, Gerald English and Ivor Pritchard.

182. To members and regulars of Llanhilleth Institute, these two will easily be recognized as Chairman Billy (Shilling) Smith making a presentation to Club Secretary Tom Price.

183. During wartime, amongst the many essential tasks that needed to be given foremost attention was the maintenance of the country's railway tracks, particularly for the movement of armaments and vital materials. Women were also employed in this type of work as seen here, when the Llanhilleth Team of workers took first prize for their efforts in 1943. Lined up are H. Rogers, A. Proctor, F. Broome, B. Gough (supervisor), B. Sargeant, Doll Carey, E. Daniels, Rene ? and H. Jeffries.

184. A group of gentlemen posing for a photographer outside the Top Hotel in about 1908, the landlord at the time being Henry Lewis who held the licence here for more than twenty years. In typical Edwardian style, the attire ranges from mufflers to bowler hats and starched collars with most of the men enjoying a pipe.

185. It is quite some years since this pictures was taken of a group of carnival entrants, possibly celebrating the Coronation in June 1953. The scene is at Central Road and some readers may be able to recognize themselves or remember the day. Central Road is of course is no longer standing, it having been demolished to make way for the new road from Aberbeeg to Crumlin.

186. Garry Thomas, his wife Marjorie and mother-in-law are seen here outside their former shop in High Street Llanhilleth, the Thomas family having already been mentioned in an earlier chapter.

187. A Llanhilleth carnival float as provided by residents of Brynithel pre-fabs, portrays characters from two traditional children's comics, the Dandy and Beano. The year is 1952 and the partakers are - Mrs. Cooper (Desperate Dan), L. Sellick (Lord Snooty), Bet Buffin (Swanky Lanky), Mrs. Gilson (Dennis The Menace), Terry and Barbara Buffin (Snitch and Snatch), Jenny and Janet Howells (Biffo the Bear and Pansy Potter).

188. Brynhyfryd School Choir in 1958 and reading left to right the singers are - Back: Martin Budd, Marlene Priest, Pam Morgan, Diane Ellis, Sylvia Summers, Norma Beckington, Jennifer Tucker, Jacqueline Mathews, Ann Williams, Pat Whitlock and Denise Goff. Middle: Elwyn Jones, ?, Meryl Pope, Jean Williams, Pam Northy, Angela Thomas, June Northy, Rae Lewis, Val Neale, Deidre Jones, ? and David Smith. Front: Mary Williams, Molly Booten, Beris Bowen, Ceinwen Sheppard, Kay Donald, Sandra Howells, Carol Kimber, Ashley Benn, Rhonda Howells, Will James and Janet Harris.

COMMERCIAL ROAD BAPTIST CHURCH
LLANHILLETH

Order of Service

on the occasion of the official attendance of

Councillor Mrs. F. M. Protheroe, J.P.

Chairman of the
Abertillery Urban District Council

at DIVINE WORSHIP on

Sunday, 26th June, 1966 at 6 p.m.

Officiating Minister : Mr. B. SAVAGE
Bible College, Barry.

Organist : Mrs. G. Rogers

189. A face that should be quite familiar to local residents is that of Mrs. Florence Protheroe J.P. who was Chairman of Abertillery Urban District Council and seen here whilst in office in 1966.

190. The interior of Commercial Road Baptist Church and Reverend E.O. Jones and his wife Olwyn pose for the camera.

191. Jack Martindale, seen here with one of his assistants outside the painters and decorators shop which Jack and his wife Elsie ran for many years. The premises in Commercial Road have since been converted into a private dwelling.

192. A blustery day at Brynithel in about 1952 for Dennis and Jeanette Buffin who were photographed during the carnival event as 'The Bisto Kids'.

193. This carnival procession at Llanhilleth is from earlier times, possibly during the 1930s with the event marking the Silver Jubilee of King George V in 1935. Hopefully there may be one or two readers who are able to recognize a parent or relative in the crowd.

194. Four local senior citizens are caught taking a breather, probably after having put the world to right and from the left they are - Bill Morgan, another Bill Morgan, Eric Roberts and George Carter.

195. As already stated, in its heyday the Central Hotel was a popular venue for social events and annual dinners. Such an event is pictured here in the 1950s and there should be plenty of local faces to remember such as Arron and Iris Edwards, Fred Hewlett, Mr. Rogers, Howard and Marion Rogers, Bill Duggan, Bert (Bogsie) Woodward, Mr. Hiscott, Eileen Baber, Eddie Donald and Mr. Davies.

196. More socializing in Llanhilleth, this time outside the Belle Vue Club in 1955 and the gentlemen are - Trevor York, Tom Meek, Joe Phelps, Syrus Patton, Bill Lippett and B. Caldwell.

197. A costumed gathering outside the Walpole Hotel in the 1920s when Jesse Smart was landlord (the building's frontage having changed somewhat since). During the Depression years of the 1930s the Walpole ran a 'Slate Club', a small organisation to help the needy and destitute of the district; when war broke out in September 1939 one of the club's rules was hastily amended as follows. Rule 3 - No claims will be paid for any Accident, or Death of any Member or Member's Wife, or any Single Member or Widowed Mothers of Single Members that is arising from any act of the enemy and any member on active service will be excused from paying a quarterly fine. This was the last bit of news that locals wanted to hear after enduring years of unemployment.

198. Four lady-members of the Jazz Band with their kazoos at the ready are Mary Hewlett, Annette Carter, Beryl Davies and Lesley Watkins.

199. A souvenir photograph of the Llanhilleth Field Rovers A.F.C. taken in the park in 1958. In the back row are 'Nobby Nookes' (trainer), C. Humphries, T. Minchin, M. Brown, J. Mahoney, E. George and W. Neale. Front: W. Hancock, J. Williams, C. Chivers (captain), C. Whitlock and B. Tucker.

200. Llanhilleth Rugby Football Club was formed by local enthusiasts in the 1890s, their headquarters nowadays being the former public house The Walpole. This particular picture was taken at some earlier premises in the 1920s but unfortunately, only three names have come to light and they are - Sam Davies (5th left, back row), Cyril Selby (3rd left, middle row) and Les Dennes (1st left, front row).

201. Continuing the rugby theme and a group of supporters prepare themselves for the first leg of the journey to an International in Paris in the 1950s. Some faces known are - Glyn Lewis (2nd left), Mr. Butler (3rd), Mostyn Jayne (4th) and Cyril Selby far right.

202. Llanhilleth All Blacks are seen surrounded by cups and medals after winning the Monmouthshire Junior League three years in succession and triumphs in 1935 and '36, winning the Blaina and Abertillery Hospital Cups. Back: D. Morgan, K. Lewis, R. Belcher, B. Galton, J. Davies, J. Challenger, T. Becker, A. Maggs, C. Jones, E. Minchin, L. Morgan, R. Jones, T. Chivers, C. Hagland and B. Parry. 3rd Row: E. Lane, R. Johnson, L. Jenkins, H. Jenkins, H. Self, S. Smith, L. Preece, T. Wall, C. Morgan, A. Brown, E. Roberts and I. Jones. 2nd Row: J. Williams and A. Jones. 1st Row: V. Cook, I. Beckington, A. Jones, A. Griffiths, E. Challenger and H. Preece.

203. From more modern times, in the 1970s, are pictured some more local sportsmen, and left to right they are - W. Hancock, J. Sellick, K. Morris, E. Bennett, A. Harris and A. Whitlock. Middle: A. Watkins, D. Bryan, P. Lapure, P. Bryan, G. Williams, D. Jayne and C. O'Brien. Front: M. Musto, G. Beach, P. Brittain, N. Dennis, L. Watkins, L. Brittain and T. Rogers.

204. Learning the skills of football must begin at an early age, as will be noted in this photograph of Llanhilleth Juniors in the 1996-7 season. Left to right, the boys are - Back: J. Dean, G. Hillier, G. Jones, T. Evans, C. Parsons, L. Yates, J. Bargh, R. Mitchell and K. Evans. Front: R. Crees, N. Morgan, A. Torrence, J. Breakwell, G. Jones, R. Penn and G. Thomas.

205. The Council Leader and her husband are the guests of honour here at an opening ceremony at Llanhilleth Bowls Club. In the back row are M. Bartlett, P. Keeling, M. Hart, H. Morgan, O. Meek, G. Price, G. Wilshire, J. Pettet, M. Edwards, C. Webley, A. Chivers, F. Johnson, B. Jones, C. Jones, M. Blanche, R. Jenkins, M. Booton and R. Rowlands. Front: B. Green, C. Jones, B. Broome, E. Hill and J. Griffiths.

206. A memorable occasion is recorded in this photograph taken at the cricket club's annual dinner and dance held at the Gwern Vale Manor Hotel Crickhowell. A presentation is being made by Phil Maggs to Arthur Sargeant, to mark his retirement from the game and in recognition of forty years service as a player.

207. The players on the pitch in 1967 are as follows - Robert Ashmead, Gerald Dyke, Arthur Martin, Ken Musto, Arthur Sargeant, Philip Bryan, Ernie Dyke, Derek Butcher (Wicket Keeper), Phil Woodland, Norman Morgan (Newport and Wales Rugby International), Phil Maggs (Captain) and Ken Hall.

208. The boys are pictured in 1996 when they were runners-up in the South Wales Conference Alliance First Division and they are - Standing: Phil Maggs (Sec.), Gwyn Davies, Malcolm Smith, Darren Protheroe, Chris Townsend (Capt.), David Wilcox and Arthur Sargeant (Chairman). Kneeling: Shane Jones, Craig Lewis, Jonathan Dalton, Andrew Watkins, Philip Blackmore, Mike Smith and Gareth Hawkins.

The game of cricket has been played in Llanhilleth for more than a century, the earliest known photograph showing a team playing Ynysddu in 1898. The club's first pitch was on ground known to locals as 'Joby's Field', now the site of a factory. At one time the River Ebbw flowed through the park, but in 1926, the course was altered to allow better use of the land; looking carefully from an elevated position, one can still follow the river's original route.

Many names can be recorded as long-serving and skilful cricketers, such as the Rogers family with brothers Oliver and George commencing after the 1914-18 war, the tradition carrying on with sons Oliver Jnr., Walter, and Ray with nephews Dennis and Stephen to follow.

In 1928, Abertillery were champions of the Second Div. East and Llanhilleth, Second Div. East - B, in the South Wales and Mon League, thus a challenge match was arranged between the two sides to be played in Abertillery Park. The game nevertheless did not run smoothly and with Abertillery batting first, their man was quickly bowled by Alf Lewis. However, the batsman immediately appealed that he was not ready and to some disbelief, the umpire ruled in his favour. When Llanhilleth's turn came to bat, with Alf Lewis at the crease, he was clean bowled but immediately appealed that he too was not ready. This time the umpire ruled against and Alf, under the strongest protest, was given out. This little incident led to the secretary, Oliver Rogers, declaring that never again would Llanhilleth play Abertillery in the park. That situation remained deadlocked for many years until new secretary Phil Maggs eventually declared a truce.

The Llanhilleth club still flourishes with many successes to its credit, too many to mention with the support of two typical stalwarts - Phil Maggs who received the Dilys Thorne Trophy for outstanding services to the sport, and an unsung hero by the name of Arthur Sargeant.

209. An essential part of Brynithel Community Centre is the catering department and the ladies are pictured here at the official opening. They are - Mrs. Sweet, Mrs. B. Rosser, Mrs. J. Bobbett, Mrs. C. Hall, Mrs. B. Pettet, Mrs. G. Dykes, I. Roberts, C. Shepard, B. Watkins, D. Wanklyn, Mrs. Haines, A. Read, G. Read and Mrs. P. Maggs.

210. Mothercraft at Brynithel Community Centre is recorded in this photograph from 1968 with infants who will now be in their thirties. Pictured are Mrs. M. Pritchard and daughter Denise, Mrs. B. Pettet with son Philip, Nurses Preece and Stephens, Mrs. E. Edwards with daughter Jane and Mrs. S. Dewfall with daughter Gina.

211. Penygraig Terrace was the setting for some fiftieth-anniversary celebrations of Victory In Europe Day, May 1995. The gentleman at the back, sporting his medals is Mr. Tom Parfitt who served in the 8th Army during the war.

212. The occasion is the opening of an Autumn Fayre at Brynithel by the local doctor's wife, Mrs. Reddy. Stood left to right are - M. Jones, M. Whelton, Mrs. Reddy and her daughter, D. Carter and M. Davies.

213. The season for this Brynithel rugby team photo-call is 1981-82 and the players and followers include, from left to right - Back: H. Hewings (Chairman), D. Jayne, E. Newman, B. Pidgeon, M. Phillips, S. Jones, C. Jarrett, T. Minchen, R. Challenger, N. Morgan, M. Fraser and S. Challenger. Middle: J. Broom, B. Green, P. Pratley, S. Hewings (Capt.), M. Peck, A. Lane and P. Wallace. Front: C. Randall, M. Hale, N. Thomas and R. Stonuary.

214. The Carnival Queen with her court of boys and girls. Back: J. Tranter and S. Tingle. Middle: M. Dix, unknown, S. Hall (Queen), Ms. Yendle and E. Reece. Front: D. Lloyd, M. Grove, Master Dix and A. Jeffreys.

215. Bryn Terrace and Bryn Crescent residents with their carnival float 'Snow White and The Seven Dwarfs' in about 1972. Snow White is played by J. Dewfall, The Prince - J. Hall, The Wicked Queen - A. Jeffreys, Fairy - M. Hancock and the dwarfs are T. Parker, A. Jeffreys, D. Martin, A. Lane and J. Rudge.

216. The carnival novelty football team and most of their names have been traced as follows. Back: Unknown, C. Stonuary, unknown, D. Carter, B. Watkins, E. Lane, unknown, O. Parsons, J. Webb, K. Williams and P. Deacon. Front: M. Whelton, M. Young, J. Inch, B. Pettet, P. Bevan, H. Darlington, L. Darlington and R. Overfield.

217. A Brynithel street tea party with a Welsh theme which may be celebrating the Investiture of The Prince of Wales in 1969. The children, left to right, are Alyson Jeffreys, Alun Jeffreys, Melanie Hancock and Susan Parker.

218. Here are half a dozen local happy campers in the fields at Brynithel in 1938 who can be identified left to right as follows - H. Carter, G. Parsons, T. Parsons, A. Carter, G. Hallet and B. Rathbone.

219. A proud moment for Llanhilleth and Brynithel Girl Guides Troop when they celebrated the awarding of three Queen's Guide Certificates. From the left are - Miss S. Davies (Guide Commissioner), Kay Edwards, Jane Howells and Julie Dewfall (Guides), Mrs. Jean Pritchard and Mrs. Christine Budd (Guide Leaders).

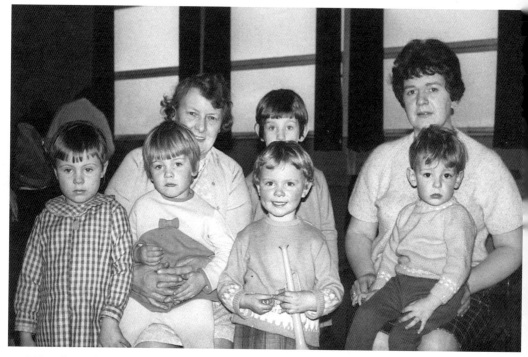

220. Saturday playtime at the centre and Mrs. Rudge (Auntie Queenie) and Mrs. Pettet are in charge of the following children - K. Maggs, H. Pettet, P. Pettet, A. Pearce and A. Pettet.

221. These glamorous ladies all belong to Brynithel Ladies Choir and are seated with their conductor Cyril Morgan. A number of names have been traced as at the time of printing and they include Mrs. Hale, Emily Lane, Mr. Earl, Mrs. Carter, Joan Parfitt, Edna Lane, Glad Jones, Muriel Edwards, Brenda ?, Iris Lane, Ginny Parsons, Blod Taylor and Joyce Hill.

222. The final photograph in the book portrays a group of local ladies of all ages and is testament to the strong community spirit that still exists in these parts. There are forty-eight faces to be seen here so space has prevented the printing of their names. However, readers will undoubtedly be able to provide most of them without any assistance from the authors on this occasion.

Acknowledgements

Acknowledgements are due to the undermentioned who kindly loaned some of their ow
photographs for inclusion in this book. Sincere apologies are extended to anyone who m
have been inadvertently omitted.

Aberbeeg R.F.C., Mr. D. Adams, Mr. Baynham, Mrs. M. Bevan, Mrs. P. Bevan, Mrs. J
Birchmore, Mrs. B. Buffin, Mrs. D. Carter, Mr. G. Carter, Mrs. P. Carter, Mr. N. Challeng
Mrs. M. Collier, Mr. T. Creed, Mr. C. Daniels, Mr. T. Day, Mr. M. Evans, Mrs. J. Fowler, M
M. Friend, Mr. G. Galloway, Mr. and Mrs. Griffiths, Mr. C. Hill, Mrs. R. Howells, Mr. I
Johnson, Mr. Bill Jones, Mrs. M. Jones, Mr. A. Kimber, Mr. D. Kimber, Mr. and Mrs.
Keeling, Mr. K. Lane, Mrs. J. Leddington, Mr. G. Legge, Mrs. L. Lewis, Mr. M. Lewis, Mr
T. Lewis, Mrs. M. Lowman, Mr. P. Maggs, Mrs. I. Mahoney, Mr. Ted Meredith, Mrs. L. Morri
Mr. and Mrs. M. Neads, Mr. Palmer, Janet Parry, Mrs. O. Parsons, Mrs. B. Pettet, Mr.
Phelps, Rev. R. Prescott, Mrs. K. Pritchard, Mr. B. Smith, Mr. E. Thomas, Mrs. J. Thoma
Mr. T. Tucker, Mr. D. Warren, Mr. D. Watkins, Mr. J.R. Webb, Mr. and Mrs. J. Wells, Mrs. M
Wheeler, Mrs. S. Winmill, Mr. and Mrs. Wixey.

Below is a selection of further titles available. Please send stamp to the Publishers for a detailed catalogue.